DK READERS

LEARNING
pre-level
1
TO READ

Petting Zoo

A Dorling Kindersley Book

 What kind of animal

A Note to Parents and Teachers

DK READERS is a compelling reading programme for children. The programme is designed in conjunction with leading literacy experts, including Cliff Moon M.Ed., who has spent many years as a teacher and teacher educator specializing in reading. Cliff Moon has written more than 0 books for children and teachers. He is series editor to ollins Big Cat.

Beautiful illustrations and superb full-colour photographs mbine with engaging, easy-to-read stories to offer a fresh proach to each subject in the series. Each DK READER is guaranteed to capture a child's interest while developing his or her reading skills, general knowledge, and love of reading.

The five levels of DK READERS are aimed at different reading abilities, enabling you to choose the books that are exactly right for your child:

Pre-level 1: Learning to read
Level 1: Beginning to read
Level 2: Beginning to read alone
Level 3: Reading alone
Level 4: Proficient readers

The "normal" age at which a child begins to read can be anywhere from three to eight years old. Adult participation through the lower levels is very helpful for providing encouragement, discussing storylines and sounding out unfamiliar words.

No matter which level you select, you are h learn to r learn!

6 756 838 000

LONDON, NEW YORK, MUNICH,
MELBOURNE, AND DELHI

Series Editor Deborah Lock
Designer Jacqueline Gooden
Art Director Martin Wilson
Pre-production Francesca Wardell
Jacket Designer Natalie Godwin

Reading Consultant
Cliff Moon M.Ed.

First published in Great Britain by
Dorling Kindersley Limited
80 Strand, London WC2R 0RL

ISBN: 978-1-40938-175-4

Colour reproduction by Colourscan, Singapore
Printed and bound in China by L.Rex Printing Co., Ltd.

The publisher would like to thank the following for their kind permission to
reproduce their photographs:
(Key: a-above; b-below/bottom; c-centre; f-far; l-left; r-right; t-top)
3 **Getty Images:** Asia Images. 4 **Corbis:** Peter Burian (c); Thomas Marent /
Visuals Unlimited (tl). **Getty Images:** Art Wolfe / Stone (b). 5 **Corbis:** DLILLC
(tr); Visuals Unlimited (c). **6-7 Getty Images:** Asia Images. 6 **Photolibrary:**
Jurgen & Christine Sohns / FLPA (br). 7 **Corbis:** Thomas Marent. / Visuals
Unlimited (t). **Getty Images:** Daniel Berehulak / Staff / Getty Images News
(br). **Photolibrary:** Stockbrokerxtra Images (bc). 8 **Corbis:** Thomas Marent /
Visuals Unlimited (br). 9 **Corbis:** Thomas Marent / Visuals Unlimited (br).
Getty Images: Luciano Candisani / Minden Pictures (c). **Photolibrary:** Terry
Whittaker / FLPA (bc). 10 **Dreamstime.com:** Lasse Kristensen (c). **Getty
Images:** Creative Crop / Digital Vision (cr); Ultra.F / Digital Vision (cb). 11
Getty Images: Rubberball / Erik Isakson. **Photolibrary:** Stockbrokerxtra Images
(bc). 12-13 **Photolibrary:** Juniors Bildarchiv. 13 **Getty Images:** Pete Mcbride /
National Geographic (bl). **Photolibrary:** Juergen und Christine Sohns (crb). 14
Getty Images: Gerry Ellis / Minden Pictures (c). 15 **Corbis:** Herbert Kehrer (br).
Getty Images: Ingo Arndt / Minden Pictures. **Photolibrary:** Cyril Ruoso (bl).
16-17 **Getty Images:** Piotr Naskrecki / Minden Pictures. 16 **Getty Images:** SA
Team / Foto Natura / Minden Pictures (bl); Kevin Schafer / Minden Pictures
(br). 17 **Getty Images:** Stan Osolinski / Oxford Scientific (br). **Photolibrary:**
Juniors Bildarchiv (bl). 18 **Getty Images:** Reinhard Dirscherl / WaterFrame (bl).
18-19 **Photolibrary:** Luiz C Marigo. 19 **Getty Images:** Reinhard Dirscherl /
WaterFrame (bc); Claus Meyer / Minden Pictures (bl). 20 **Science Photo
Library:** Chris Hellier (clb). 20-21 **Alamy Images:** Chris Hellier. 21 **Getty
Images:** Christian Kober / Robert Harding World Imagery (bc); Thomas
Marent / Minden Pictures (br). **Photolibrary:** Nick Garbutt (bl). 22 **Getty
Images:** Keren Su / Photodisc (t); Tier Und Naturfotografie J & C Sohns / The
Image Bank (bl). 23 **Getty Images:** Ben Cranke / The Image Bank; Lori Epstein
/ National Geographic (br). 24 **Corbis:** Peter Burian (c). **Getty Images:** Brooke
Whatnall / National Geographic (bl). 25 **Corbis:** Anup Shah (bl). **Getty
Images:** Fuse (br); Copyright Tony Franco / Flickr. 26-27 **Getty Images:** Visuals
Unlimited, Inc. / John Abbott. 26 **Photolibrary:** Michel & Christine
Denis-Huot (t). 27 **Corbis:** DLILLC (br). **Getty Images:** Steve Allen /
Photodisc (bc); Ben Cranke / The Image Bank (bl). 28-29 **Getty Images:** Sune
Wendelboe / Lonely Planet Images. 28 **Corbis:** Martin Harvey (bl). 29 **Corbis:**
Darrell Gulin (bl). **Photolibrary:** Christian Heinrich (bc); Keith Levit (br). 30
Dreamstime.com: Robert Wisdom (bl). **Getty Images:** Fotosearch. 31 **Corbis:**
Herbert Kehrer (cb). **Photolibrary:** Berndt Fischer (t); National Geographic
Society (br). 32 **Corbis:** Tim Davis (cb); DLILLC (ca); Oliver Lassen (b).
Dreamstime.com: Michael Lynch (t).
Jacket images: Front: naturepl.com: Nick Garbutt

All other images © Dorling Kindersley
For further information see: www.dkimages.com

Discover more at
www.dk.com

We are at the
petting zoo.

do you see here?

We are petting
a drowsy donkey.

 donkeys

ear

hoof

We are walking two baby llamas.

llamas

lead

I am brushing a pony's coat.

mane

 ponies

 pigs

I am picking up
a little pink pig.

snout

hoof

hen

 chicks

14

I am carrying
a soft yellow chick.

chick

 stick insects

leaf

stick insect

I am holding
a green stick insect.

 frogs

I am watching
a beady-eyed frog.

Ribbit! Ribbit!

toe

It is mealtime now.
I give the woolly lamb
some milk.

 lambs

wool

I am feeding
a hungry rabbit.

ear

carrot

rabbits

This fluffy guinea pig
is nibbling a leaf.

 guinea pigs

whiskers

claws

The white goose wants a snack.

  geese

gosling

bill

feathers

goats

This long-horned
goat is eating
his lunch.

horn

Goodbye, animals!

It's time to go home.

Glossary

Donkey
a small horse-like animal with long ears

Frog
a short animal with long back legs

Goose
a large white bird with a long beak

Llama
a large woolly animal from South America

Stick insect
a long thin insect that looks like a stick